PEOPLE IN COSTUME

The 1970s and 1980s

JENNIFER RUBY

1978

1987

B.T. Batsford Ltd · London

© Jennifer Ruby 1994
First Published 1994

Typeset
and printed by Colorcraft, Hong Kong
for the Publishers
B.T. Batsford Ltd
4 Fitzhardinge Street
London W1H 0AH

A CIP catalogue record for this book is available from the
British Library.

ISBN 0 7134 7218 9

1978

CONTENTS

1985

INTRODUCTION

The 1970s, 1980s and early 1990s were an exciting time in the fashion world. For the first time in history, there was no clear idea of what was fashionable. Instead, people wore what they wanted to and the feeling was 'anything goes'.

Important influences on fashion during this period included famous people like pop and T.V. stars and Princess Diana, the strange, aggressive look of punk and the ethnic look that came from foreign cultures. There was also a nostalgia for the past and many people looked back into history to find ideas for clothes which meant that many fashions from previous years reappeared.

Let us now imagine that it is 1970 and meet Emma, a young housewife.

"Hello, I used to be a hippie in the 1960s and I still like to wear long skirts made from pretty materials. Today I am wearing a very short, tight fitting jacket over a full, long-sleeved blouse with a matching ankle length skirt. My cap is crocheted and on my feet I am wearing sandals with platform soles. I also love to wear clothes by Laura Ashley as in the picture.

Now I am going to take you on a journey through the 1970s, 1980s and early 1990s so that you can meet many different characters and compare their clothes and lifestyles."

1971

1972: MINIS AND MAXIS

We will begin our journey on the streets of London, where there are a variety of different styles of clothing to be seen. Mini skirts and maxi skirts are both popular, as you can see from these two contrasting styles.

Susan is wearing a mini dress that has been designed by Mary Quant. Her shoes have platform soles and her hair is worn in flick-ups.

Her friend Jackie has on a very different outfit designed by Brian Baker. It has lots of lace, frills and flounces and gives her a gypsy look. Her hair is worn long and curly.

Which of these two designs do you prefer? Which do you think would be the most practical to wear?

Susan

Jackie

LONG AND SHORT

Here are three of Susan's other friends wearing contrasting outfits.

Jane is wearing green hot pants with a matching blouse and platform-soled shoes. Linda has on pink dungarees and Brenda is wearing a woollen trouser suit with a matching cap.

Which is the most practical outfit?

MEN'S CLOTHES

Here is Susan's boyfriend Richard and his friend Guy. They are wearing typical outfits from the early 1970s.

Richard has on a patterned jumper which is quite short and has a deep rib at the waist. His trousers are very wide and are called Oxford bags. They are similar to those worn by young men in the 1920s. He also has on a plain shirt, a bow-tie, a trilby hat and shoes with platform soles.

Richard

Guy is wearing a corduroy trouser suit with a patterned, V-necked jumper, a plain shirt and boots. Guy's trousers are not as wide as Richard's, they are flared from the knee and are called bell bottoms.

Guy

1974: THE COUNTRY LOOK

Richard and Susan often like to spend time in the country away from the hustle and bustle of London. On the left you can see them relaxing at Richard's parents' home.

Richard is wearing a gilet, (quilted waistcoat), over a yellow sweatshirt, corduroy trousers, boots and a scarf.

Susan has on a cream coloured jumper, green corduroy trousers and matching hat and boots. They have just returned from a long walk.

Richard's sister Genna is wearing what is called the 'layered look'. She has on a brown corduroy dress, a knitted coat, two scarves and a matching hat and mittens.

WINTER WARMTH

Here are Genna, Susan and Richard on their way to the local town to do some shopping.

Genna is wearing a culotte suit, a plain shirt, a beret and leather boots. She is carrying a large leather shoulder bag.

Susan is wearing a woollen midi-length coat with a shoulder cape, a polo-necked sweater, leather boots and a pretty hat. Richard has on a long woollen overcoat, a polo-necked sweater, wool trousers, a cap and a long scarf.

Genna

Susan

Richard

THE DENIM CRAZE

By the 1970s, jeans had become very popular as casual wear with both the old and young. In the local town we meet lots of people wearing denim, as it is such a comfortable fabric.

Geoff is wearing a denim jacket and matching jeans. His sister Claire, (opposite), is wearing jeans with turn-ups, a striped T-shirt and red boots. Sometimes, when she goes out with her friend Lisa, Claire likes to wear her favourite dungarees, which have a Micky Mouse motif on the front pocket.

What has happened to the width of trousers?

rubber-soled denim shoe, designed to go with jeans

1976: PUNK

One very important influence on fashion in the 1970s was the arrival of Punk. It seemed very aggressive, violent and ugly at first, as young people wore black clothes that were tattered and torn, pierced holes in their ears and noses and covered themselves with chains and tattoos.

If we return to London we can meet Mick and Tina, who are Punks. Mick has his head shaved at the sides and the hair on top has been grown and is held up in spikes with the aid of soap. This is called a Mohican hairstyle. He is wearing a black sleeveless T-shirt, jeans and a leather bracelet with studs. He has one pierced ear.

His girlfriend Tina is wearing a black floral shirt over a black skirt, torn net fingerless gloves that reach to the elbow, and she has chains around her neck. Her hair is soaped to make it stand out and she has painted black circles around her eyes.

Why do you think people found Punk frightening?

Mick

Tina

1977: PUNK CHIC

In 1977, a famous clothes designer called Zandra Rhodes took some of the Punk ideas and used them in her collection of designs for that year. She embroidered tatters with gold thread, used gold safety pins, beads and many colours and suddenly the punk that had been ugly became something chic.*

Zandra is pictured here with multi-coloured hair. She has painted her body blue and pink and is wearing a dress that is covered with beads and embroidery. On the opposite page you can see a punk wedding dress and two punk T-shirts.

Suddenly, everyone wanted to copy what had at first seemed bizarre and outrageous.

* Chic - means stylish and elegant.

1981: TWO FAMOUS LADIES

We will now move forward to the 1980s. Here you can see two famous ladies from that decade. Both had a lot of influence on fashion, although they are so very different.

The pop star Madonna deliberately set out to shock people with her outrageous fashions. She wore tight-fitting under-wear, corsets and black tights on stage and started a fashion for the 'bustier' top. Once, when unable to find anything to tie her hair back with, she used an old pair of tights and immediately started another fashion trend!

Princess Diana captured the heart of the nation when she married Prince Charles in 1981. She did a lot to boost the millinery* trade by wearing lovely hats to complement her many outfits. Women throughout the world tried to copy her looks and fashions.

Both these ladies attracted attention and were copied by thousands. Can you think of any more famous people who influenced fashion?

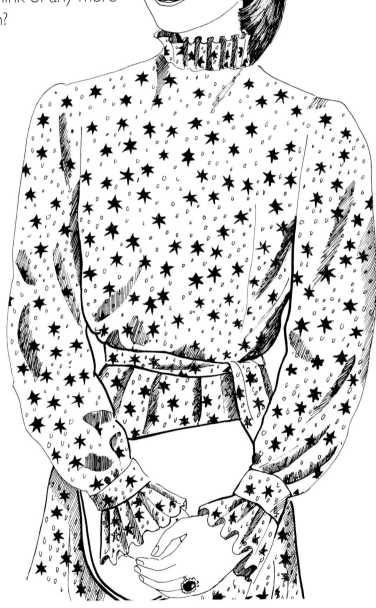

* Millinery - a Milliner is someone who makes hats.

DANDIES AND PRINCES

A dandy is a man who is overly concerned with his appearance. The two men pictured here might be called dandies because of their flamboyant* style of dress.

On the right you can see the pop star Prince, who is wearing a ruffled shirt and a brightly coloured and tight-fitting suit with decorative buttons. Can you find his bracelet and the pearls on his suit? He is also wearing eye liner and make-up.

* Flamboyant means extravagant, showy and colourful.

This is David, who is wearing an equally colourful outfit consisting of a patchwork silk jacket with lace cuffs, a blue shirt, purple trousers and boots. Both men have permed hair.

Can you find out about a famous dandy from the nineteenth century called Beau Brummell?

1985: STREET STYLE

One interesting feature of the 1980s was the influence of 'street style'. Street fashions originated with young people and were called 'anti-style': this meant that the traditional rules of taste and fashion were deliberately broken in order to produce original outfits. (Punk was an example of street style in the 1970s.)

Sylvie and Chrissie have each adopted an original way of dressing. Their clothes are what we might call 'anti-style' because they are unusual and, to some people, they would seem distasteful.

Sylvie is wearing a smart denim jacket with two brooches for decoration but she has teamed this with a pair of very ripped jeans. Sometimes she patches her jeans with un-matching fabric as in the small picture below.

torn jeans, patched on the inside

Chrissie is wearing an oversize mac with lace cuffs, a black tunic over a lace-edged miniskirt and black tights. Her hair is frizzed and wild.

Can you design an unusual outfit that combines items of clothes not normally worn together?

THE ETHNIC INFLUENCE

Another important fashion influence during the 1980s came from various ethnic groups and traditional national costumes. Many of the shapes, patterns and exciting colour mixes that occurred were based on traditional designs from other countries. For example, there were cheesecloth* and muslin* skirts and tops from India, Russian-look peasant skirts, chunky jewellery from Africa, leather bags from Morocco, silver from the Middle East and Fair Isle pattern sweaters from Scotland. There was also a renewed interest in handicrafts like knitting and crochet.

This is Alma, who is wearing a hand-crocheted blue dress. Her hair is frizzed and she has on startling red lipstick and nail polish.

Some of her friends are also pictured here. They are wearing outfits that show the influence of other countries.

Alma

* Muslin is a fine cotton fabric
* Cheesecloth is a loosely woven cotton fabric

1987: EAST MEETS WEST

The word 'couture' means high fashion designing and dressmaking. Zaineb Alam was an Asian couturier who wanted to attract both Eastern and Western women with her clothes designs. She set up a company called Zee Zee and used the eastern look as a basis for her designs. She produced beautiful clothes that could be worn by women both from the east and the west.

Other Asian designers followed suit and produced clothes like those pictured here. This was good news to many Asian girls who had been born in the West and found themselves torn between their traditional clothes and the fashions of the country in which they lived.

YUPPIES

'Yuppie' was a word used in the 1980s to describe a young, dynamic, professional person who was career-minded and energetic.

Geoff and Anita could be described as yuppies. They have high-powered jobs and earn and spend a great deal of money.

Geoff is wearing a double-breasted jacket, a casual shirt and loose, baggy, cotton trousers called chinos.

Anita is wearing a yellow suit with padded shoulders and a pencil slim skirt. She has a wide leather belt at her waist and carries a matching leather case. She is holding a shawl.

This kind of look is called 'power dressing'. Can you think why this might be?

THE FITNESS CRAZE

Geoff and Anita are very keen on keeping fit and often work out with their friends Gabrielle and John. Here you can see John out running. He is training for the London marathon and is wearing a track suit and trainers.

Gabrielle is in the gym. She is wearing a leotard, tights and leg warmers.

Throughout history, sports clothes have often become high fashion. This happened in the 1980s, when many items of sports wear suddenly became very fashionable. For example, track suits were often worn in the street or even to parties and people could be seen shopping in colourful cycling shorts and tops.

LYCRA SENSATION

The health and fitness boom of the late 1970s and 1980s meant that many people were fitter than they had ever been. It became fashionable to show off healthy bodies in figure-hugging fabrics like lycra, which stretched to fit like a second skin.

On the right you can see Gabrielle in a lycra top and skirt and Alma is pictured wearing a lycra mini dress.

On the far right, Anita is wearing fashionable cycling shorts and matching top.

Can you think of some items of fashionable clothes that we wear today that were originally meant for sportswear?

AT THE SEASIDE

More and more people also took up outdoor sports. Activities like windsurfing, sailing, canoeing and cycling were popular.

Tom and Nadine often like to spend a day at the seaside. Here they are enjoying the outdoor life.

Both are wearing waterproof cotton jackets and denim shirts. Nadine has on stretch trousers and moccasins. Tom is wearing thick cotton trousers and boots.

1992: FRENCH LEAVE

During the early 1990s there was increased trade and travel between countries in the European Community. Inevitably, fashions also crossed the channel.

Here is Gabrielle, who frequently travels to Paris with her job. You can see the French influence in her outfits.

On the left, she is wearing a beret, a stretch stripy T-shirt and leggings. On the right she is wearing a fitted cotton jacket, jodhpurs and boots.

Can you find out more about fashions in E.C. countries?

HAIRSTYLES AND ACCESSORIES

Here are some hairstyles and accessories from the period covered by this book. Can you look at the dates beside the accessories and work out which character they might have belonged to?

two-tone hairstyle, 1979

1986

woollen hat and matching gloves, 1974

a hairstyle called "The Brush", 1972

hair "extensions", 1980 (false hair is woven into existing hair to make it longer)

chunky jewellery from Africa, 1990

black leather and silver belt, 1985

lace-up boots, made of canvas, 1970

suede shoes, 1979

walking/casual shoes, 1983

leather driving gloves, 1980

leather hand bag, 1976

platform sole shoes, 1976

small leather bag and purse, 1984

hat with fur trim, flower-patterned scarf, 1975

man's slip-on shoe, 1974

CHILDREN'S CLOTHES

Children's clothes were very bright, colourful and comfortable during the 1970s, 1980s and early 1990s. Here are some examples.

1976

1984

1990

1989

1972

FASHION REVIVALS

1989, 1950s
style twin-set
and leggings

1993, The 1960s Hippie
Look - shirt tied at the
midriff, cotton skirt

To revive something means to bring it back to life. During the late 1980s and early 1990s there were many 'new' fashions that were not new at all but were revivals from the past.

Let us finish our journey through the 1970s, 1980s and early 1990s by looking at some revived fashions. Can you make any predictions for the fashions you might be wearing in a few years time?

1988, 1950s hairstyles

1985

men's all-in-one underwear in the style of the 1930s

1993

platform soles, from the 1970s

1993, flared trousers from the 1960s

GLOSSARY AND INDEX

A WORD GAME

Now that you have read the book, see if you can find an outfit that could be described by each one of these words:

CHIC, STYLISH, ELEGANT, FLAMBOYANT, ANTI-STYLE, BIZARRE, SPORTY